S. M. CLAYTON

The Easy Guide to Resume Writing

An HR Executive's Secrets to Winning Resumes at Any Level

First edition

This book was professionally typeset on Reedsy.
Find out more at reedsy.com

Contents

1

Introduction

Resumes! The resume is a document that can inspire both creativity and at the same time create a fair amount of stress and fatigue. As a Chief Human Resources Officer with over 20 years of HR experience, I have heard just about every question and complaint that developing a resume can create. What should I write? How long should it be? What format should I use? Should I use bullets, or paragraphs? Can I use a ghostwriter or automated tool? What action words should I use? Why do I even need a resume?

This book will answer all these questions and more, which is something I am truly excited about. I have reviewed thousands of resumes over my career, and I felt it was time to share my unique spin on what an HR office or a hiring manager truly looks for in a resume. I am really excited to pull back the veil on what makes a good resume.

Turning Dread into Desire

Even though I work in the HR world, I used to dread the process of resume writing too. Resume writing can sometimes be considered by some as a necessary evil they would love to skip. What excites me most about this book is the ability to show how the resume writing process can be quite enjoyable. After all, you get to write about a topic you should know a lot about: yourself.

In this book, we will explore resume writing as more of a personal experience rather than some vague, abstract exercise. In the pages that follow we will take what is viewed by some as an antiquated pre-employment requirement, and flip that into how resume writing really puts you in the driver's seat, not the employer. Your resume will become a vehicle to convey what is desirable about you and what you bring to the table as a prospective employee.

I designed this book to be easy to read. It is important to me that the tips and tricks I share with you will be easy to apply as well. In the pages that follow, I will define what makes up a well-crafted resume. I will offer you insights from both the HR point of view as well as the view of you as the writer. Together we will explore differences between resumes in different sectors. We will explore how to organize your resume and make it "pop".

I will share ways you can craft your resume to stand out regardless of your knowledge and experience base. Through this book, you will gain a keen understanding of what employers look for in a potential employee. More importantly, you will learn ways you can surprise them with info they didn't think they needed or wanted to know.

It's All About You

This book is designed to transform the resume writing process into a storytelling opportunity on one of the most unique stories the world has known. That uniqueness is you. What company doesn't want someone that is one of a kind? The resume is a short story about how your professional experiences make you not only the best fit for the job you want, but also coveted.

This book is not designed to be a long winded attempt to dazzle you with how much I know about resumes and how to create them. I will share some of that dazzling knowledge with you, but what is more important to me is making sure you receive practical tips that you can use to create a winning resume.

Key Point #1: The true purpose of resume writing is to focus your efforts on ways you can unlock, uncover, and unleash your unique story.

More importantly, I will show you easy ways you can present your story in compelling ways that will leave employers wanting to know you more, which means they will want to interview you and potentially hire you.

I hope that reading this book helps you to experience how fun and easy resume writing can be. My goal in writing this book is that you discover that you are a pretty incredible person, and the right employer will see that, want that, and chase after that to make you a part of their organization.

2

What is a Resume and Why Do I Need It?

Resumes: A Brief History

The word resume comes from the French language meaning "to summarize." Some historians trace the concept of one of history's earliest resumes back to the late 1400s and Leonardo da Vinci. As many of us know, da Vinci painted the Mona Lisa and the Last Supper with Jesus and His disciples. He is credited in drawing the designs for what could have been a helicopter. While he had a number of interests and talents, da Vinci was not always so world renowned. In what some call one of history's first resumes, da Vinci wrote a brief letter that contained information about his skills and several things he believed he could do for the city of Milan as he was looking around the city for work.

Fast forward to around the mid 20th century in the United States, resumes began to take hold as a formal document used by professionals as part of their effort to share the job experience they had. These documents could be very long. Length was often used to convey expertise.

The longer your resume often meant you had more experiences. More experiences meant that employers may have been more inclined to hire you.

In an analog age, the resume was the document a person developed to convey authority in their line of work. As we moved into the digital and information ages, the page length of resumes began to mean less and less. The creation of YouTube and personal cell phones gave prospective employees the ability to create video resumes instead of the typical paper-based document.

In the 21st century, the resume of today is about brevity and impact, bringing us essentially full circle to how the concept of a resume started in the 1400s. Suffice it to say, resumes have a long history. The core issue is that a resume is designed for one thing: effectively summarizing your professional skills and experiences to promote yourself as a professional.

Resumes vs. CVs vs. Cover Letters: Why a Resume is a Must

Resumes differ from a curriculum vitae (CV) primarily because a CV is used in academic circles to convey coursework you have completed, research you have performed, or academic papers you have authored. Resumes differ from a cover letter in that a cover letter is designed to be an appeal to the company about why they should hire you or why you want to work for a particular organization. While cover letters can be a helpful accompaniment to a resume, they should not be used as a replacement for a resume. The specific role of the resume is to summarize your job experience and/or foreshadow your job aspirations. We will talk more about job aspirations a bit later when talking about professional motivation.

The reason every professional needs a resume is that the resume's main purpose is for marketing what is unique about you and your job experiences. The reason you need a resume no matter how much experience you have or what level in the company you rise to, is because resumes are the primary tool companies use to initially assess fitness for the work you may want to do in the future.

Genius Recognizes Genius

With nearly 600 years of history, the resume is not likely to go away anytime soon. If a genius like Leonardo di Vinci believed in the power of a resume, all of us can benefit from having one. It doesn't matter if you are a Nobel Prize winning genius, a custodian mopping floors, or both...you need a resume. It doesn't matter if you are the CEO of the business, a taxi driver, a doctor in private practice...you need a resume. It doesn't matter if you are an inventor/entrepreneur, a worker on the assembly line or President of the United States...you need a resume.

You need a resume because it is the core document recognized internationally that is used to summarize who you are as a professional. No matter who you are, everyone works for someone and therefore should have a resume to explain their knowledge and skills. Employees work for their supervisor or the corporation. The CEO works for shareholders showing how they successfully lead others and increase the profitability of their company. The President works for the people's vote in hopes of being re-elected. The rideshare driver works to distinguish themselves to gain that next fare, especially in the age of Uber and Lyft. The private business owner works for their employees (the good ones anyway) and for the loyalty of customers they hope to bring through their doors.

Each of us spends a great deal of time working on something while working for someone. The resume is the place where every person can summarize what all that work means, why it is significant and market that to the world as you look to be hired by a new employer.

Key Point #2: Everyone has a story to tell, and the resume is your tool to create that story and inspire others with your unique professional story.

3

Key Sections of Your Resume

One of the frequent questions I mentioned in the introduction that I hear often is "what should I put in my resume?". I would say there are two important things you need to put into your resume: purpose and organization.

We will touch on purpose in the next chapter, so this chapter will focus on organization. Every good story needs an outline, and a resume is no different. Understanding the order in which you will touch on key areas of your professional experience is a key component to the concept of resume writing organization.

Key Point #3: Your main role as the author of your resume is to provide the resume reader a map of your professional experiences by making it easy to understand your expertise and achievements.

The reader could be an HR staffer, a supervisor, or even artificial intelligence tools and scanners. No matter who or what is doing the reading, you want to have an organized story arc about your professional experience that you want to convey to the reader. This organized story arc will help you remember key points when it comes to telling compelling stories about your experiences for the job interview.

When writing a resume, there are five key sections that I look for and that I make sure to include in my own resume.

Professional Overview and/or Statement of Objective

This section is the preamble to your resume. It is the appetizer before the main course of more detailed information about your job experiences. Keeping in mind that the audience for your resume can be varied, you need to prepare for the different types of readers you will encounter:

- Individuals that are either too busy to read
- Individuals that skim
- Individuals that only read to first page to see if they want to read more
- Artificial intelligence (AI) programs designed to look for and score you on keywords

Creating an overview section up front in your resume is important to either capture the attention of the human reader so they read more, or share information you want them to know so the reader can have highlights of the knowledge, skills, and abilities that you will go into more detail sharing when describing your work experience.

I recommend that individuals that have a minimum of 2-3 years of job experience in the field they are applying for should create a professional overview, especially if they held more than one job over the course of that 2-3 years. If you have only held one job in that three years, it may not be necessary to create a professional overview. I encourage you to include a Professional Overview so you can highlight key skills, industry buzzwords, and an achievement or award that you are proud of relating to your field (i.e. published researcher, employee of the year, feature in a professional magazine, etc.). This section should ideally be no longer than 5-7 lines. Here is an example of a professional overview:

Five years of experience in clerical, administrative, and office management. Experience providing management and leadership to 15 staff, maintaining budgeting and financial management reports for an import-export business with 3 office locations, accurate data entry and analysis ability, project management scheduling, and meeting facilitation. Skill in staff interviewing, hiring, and employee training in customer service. Proficient in English and Mandarin Chinese.

A Statement of Objective can be helpful to individuals that are seeking their first professional job or if you are seeking to change fields. If you have several years of experience and you are seeking a career field change, I would encourage you to include your Statement of Objective listed first and then share the Professional Overview summary. A Statement of Objective should also be no longer than 5-7 lines and can be as simple as the following:

I am looking to leverage my collegiate education and work experiences interacting with people to improve the public service sector. I endeavor to use my love of macroeconomic principles and my love of statistics to work for an organization that allows me to impact public policy while working for the U.S. Department of Commerce to improve business ownership among all Americans.

It is perfectly okay to ask for the type of job you want in this statement. That focus demonstrates you are attracted to the organization's mission and purpose for existing. The name of the organization in your

Statement of Objectives can always be updated depending on who you submit your resume to, or can be made more generic (i.e. working for the Federal Government, or working for a non-profit sector organization).

Job Experience

This section is the heart of your resume. This section will include the employers you have worked for and what time period you worked for them. If your resume is for a federal government or state government position, you may be required to provide salary information, the name of your supervisor, and the address of your employer as part of this section. Below you will find two visuals of how this section could begin to look in a private sector resume compared to a federal government resume, as an example:

403 Hyacinth Dr   Day Phone: 555-777-1868
Annapolis, MD 21722   Cell: 777-555-5562
E Mail: jake.reynolds@gmail.com

Jacob Reynolds

EMPLOYMENT HISTORY

Department of Commerce, National Institute of Standards and Technology (NIST)

Position: Senior HR Strategist   March 2021-May 2022

Private Sector Resume Excerpt

Jacob Reynolds

403 Hyacinth Dr
Annapolis, MD 21772
E-Mail: jake.reynolds@gmail.com

Day Phone: 555-777-1868
Cell: 777-555-1562

EMPLOYMENT HISTORY

Department of Commerce, National Institute of Standards and Technology (NIST), Office of Human Resources, 1305 Eastern Highway, Aberdeen, MD 20104, Supervisor: Jane Jones, Hours Worked: 40/week, Salary: $130,700

Federal Government Sector Resume Excerpt

Relevant Volunteer Experience

While not a typical section to include, I strongly encourage you to find ways to highlight the charitable work or pro-bono work that you have done. This section is especially important if your volunteer experiences were done consistently and demonstrate a linkage to the job skills they are seeking as part of the job I am applying for.

Another way to leverage this section is including special projects or work you took on as part of your regular job that required at least 8 hours of work per week on average but were not part of your typical work. To develop this section in your resume, you would create it just like the job experience section of your resume. I especially like this section for people who may be early in their career and don't have a lot of relevant experiences to draw from. I also like this section for individuals looking to change career fields.

For instance, I have used this section myself. I served as the chairperson for a 25-member council to improve hiring practices in the Federal government. At the time, I had never supervised anyone in my regular job, but I outlined my job duties for this role as chairperson to showcase leadership and management skills when applying for a senior executive position. I was successful and was selected for the position. After I joined the new company, one of the interviewers told me that the work I did as chairperson was really impressive and was an important factor in selecting me for the position.

Even if you haven't worked full time in a particular field, the skills you learn in volunteer positions can be transferable. If you haven't done such work, volunteering your time so you can learn or get practical exposure to learning these skills could be an important step in your effort to land a job in a new field or in upper level supervision.

Key Point #4: Having a Relevant Volunteer Work Experience section in your resume is also a great way to showcase another dimension of your personality.

These experiences can give you a set of skills and compelling stories to share in your job interview as well. This experience can set you apart from other job applicants in the process.

Education, Certifications, Special Skills

Unlike a curriculum vitae, this section is not to list every course you took in college, or even list courses that are relevant to the skills you need in the position you are applying for. This section is to list your high school completion, vocational education, college degrees, advanced degrees, or professional certifications related to the position you are interested in applying for.

If you are applying for your first job, it is okay to add your GPA, if it is significantly high (over a 3.5). This will allow you to add if you graduated cum laude, magna cum laude, or summa cum laude as an undergraduate. I would only keep that on the resume until you land your first job out of college or your advanced degree. Keep in mind that your degree becomes dated over time. No employer will really look for what level you graduated undergrad at when you are five (5) years removed from college and have more professional experiences than college experiences.

I like to place this section toward the end regardless of the level of experience that you have. If you are early in your career, putting this section first can take away the importance of any job experience you do have. No employer is going to hire you, just because you have a degree. Is it something that can distinguish you from other candidates? It sure can

Key Point #5: It is a rare circumstance that your level of education will be the sole determining factor as to why you get hired.

Remember, the resume is about taking the human reader on a unique journey. Your experiences, not your coursework, hold greater significance. Employers will place a higher value on certifications in some instances, as an example of going beyond the traditional college or advanced degree.

Certifications like Certified Public Accountant, Project Management Professional, Professional Engineer, Six Sigma (green or black belt), Executive Coach are great items to add to this section. If you are a human resources or IT professional (or desire to transition into one of these fields), there are a number of certifications that you may want to include in this section, especially if it will help set you apart from other job applicants in a professional market.

Finally, I mentioned a concept called "special skills." Typically, if you have already talked about education and certification, the only other special skill that makes a difference is speaking a foreign language.

Key Point #6: If you can speak another language and could pass an assessment that tests your fluency, put that information in your resume.

You can even change the heading to read Education, Certification, and Language Skills to call out that you have fluency in more than one language.

Awards and Recognition

A nice way to end your resume on a high note is to include a short section on any special awards or recognition you have received. This is not the section to brag about your yearly performance bonus. This section is where you can highlight if you received special commendations or accolades for going above and beyond in a particular area that were recognized outside of your current employer.

In this section I have seen people list awards given by professional associations such as Realtor of the year, for example. Maybe you received an award from a non-profit organization for your work and volunteerism. Perhaps you received a citation from your church, mosque or synagogue for your work in the community. Maybe the local, state, or federal government has acknowledged your contributions in some way.

Key Point #7: Showcasing awards demonstrates that your exper-tise is valued and recognized by entities outside of your current

office while showing a connection with a broader community that could be of interest to your prospective employer.

Sharing these awards in your resume is a great way to set yourself apart while also demonstrating your level of expertise.

4

Highlighting Your Professional Experiences

Much like when Leornardo da Vinci wrote his resume about how he could help the city of Milan, you need to determine what your purpose is for writing the resume. Some may say that the purpose is to get a job, and while this is true, that statement is an oversimplification of why you need to create a resume. The purpose or the root issue behind writing the resume is probably more important than the end goal of the resume, which is to get a job.

Understanding what your purpose is shows that you know your own value. Knowing your value while still remaining humble sparks a confidence that you can showcase to a prospective employee when you get to the job interview. Having confidence in your purpose, especially if it aligns with the organization's culture you applied for will show three key things:

- That you have direction
- That you are aligned with the culture of the organization, and
- That you can grow roots and commit to achieving company goals

Creating your Motivational Resume for a Purposeful Interview

Something that will help you find your purpose is understanding your motivation. Are you writing the resume because you want to move up in your career as a professional expert? Do you want to transition into a leadership role and be hired as a supervisor or executive? Do you want to change careers? Do you want to establish a career? Understanding your motivation can help you clarify your ultimate purpose in writing the resume. Your answer to these questions will set up your motivation and guide you on how to tailor your resume to better highlight your skills.

Knowing what you want to achieve in your career (your motivation) must be paired with some notion of the type of person you want to be when you operate in the position you are seeking (your purpose). Your motivation will help you tailor your resume for how you showcase your job knowledge and experience. Your purpose will help guide you when you get to the interview. You need to write your resume with your interview in mind.

Key point #8: Your resume is actually the script for your job interview.

Just like the resume has five major sections to help you organize how you present the unique story about your professional career, each job you choose to highlight also needs organization. You must create Skill Based Subheadings to organize your job experience and the stories you will tell in the interview.

Skill Based Subheadings

Skill based subheadings are nothing more than subheadings that highlight a key job skill or ability. The potential employer will usually talk about what they are looking for in the job announcement itself. If you are interested in a particular field, similar jobs will have requests for the same skills so you will not have to rewrite your resume every time a new job comes open. Your resume will be like an evergreen tree. If you take the time to identify the key skills and abilities needed for the type of position you want, the resume can be used over and over without the need to be changed. You can then use that subheading to create mini stories you can use in your job interview

Below I have included an example of how to use Skill Based Subheadings to organize your job experience.

403 Hyacinth Dr   Day Phone: 555-777-1868
Annapolis MD 21772   Cell: 777-555-1562
E Mail: jake.reynolds@gmail.com

Jacob Reynolds

EMPLOYMENT HISTORY

Department of Commerce, National Institute of Standards and Technology (NIST), Office of Human Resources, 1305 Eastern Highway, Aberdeen, MD 20104, Supervisor: Jane Jones, Hours Worked: 40/week, Salary: $130,700

Position: Senior HR Strategist   March 2023-Present

HR Leadership, Strategy and Vision
- Maintain leadership HR strategy and operations for 1,800 employee organization to include: labor and employee relations, talent acquisition, performance culture and learning, policy, payroll, HRIT, HR analytics, senior executive resources, HR business consultants, HR strategy, and office administration responsible for managing a $50 million annual budget used to address internal employee benefits and complete 250 hires yearly.
- Led the hiring backlog reduction team by completing at least 500 hiring actions for two consecutive years, accomplishing a feat that has not been done for 20 years

Program Management
- Created a culture of project planning in HR for the first time by leading the creation of the HR office's first project management office to ensure on-time delivery of HR tools and services resulting in the first scheduled list of product releases for supervisory use

Skill Based Subheading Sample

Set up skill based subheadings for each job individually. You do not want to mix this job and another job under the same subheading as it will be a recipe for confusion for the reader. Just focus on one job, the subheadings you want to create, organize your related job experience bullets (more to come on this) under the correct subheading, then move to the next job in your resume and do the same thing for that job.

If you have determined what your motivation is for the resume, you can use that motivation to get creative about the types of skills that position needs to be successful. If you are applying for a supervisory position, maybe you create a section in one or all of your jobs on Leading People or Leading Change. If you are applying to be a project manager, perhaps you create subheading for Strategic Planning or Financial and Resource

Management as examples. If you are an engineer, perhaps you have a subheading on Innovation or Data Analytics and Visualization.

The key is to think about what skills you have that will make you successful in the position you want, and then highlight how you are already doing those things in your resume. This will allow you to show how you already have the skills, even if you have not done the job yet.

When I get stuck on what skills I may need to showcase for a position, my favorite website to go to is a web site linked to the U.S Department of Labor called O*NET: www.onetonline.org.

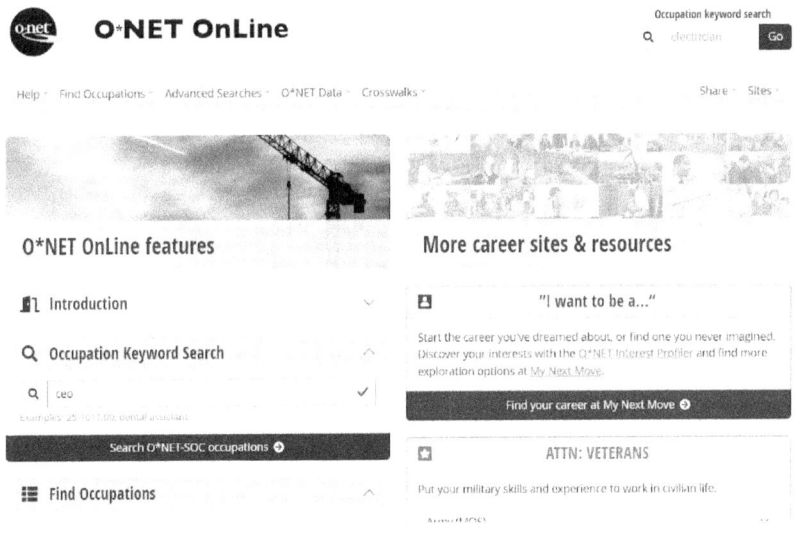

*O*NET Online Home page*

Once on this site you can search thousands of positions and get insights on great skill based subheadings. In the picture above, I have done a search to be a Chief Executive Officer and received the following results.

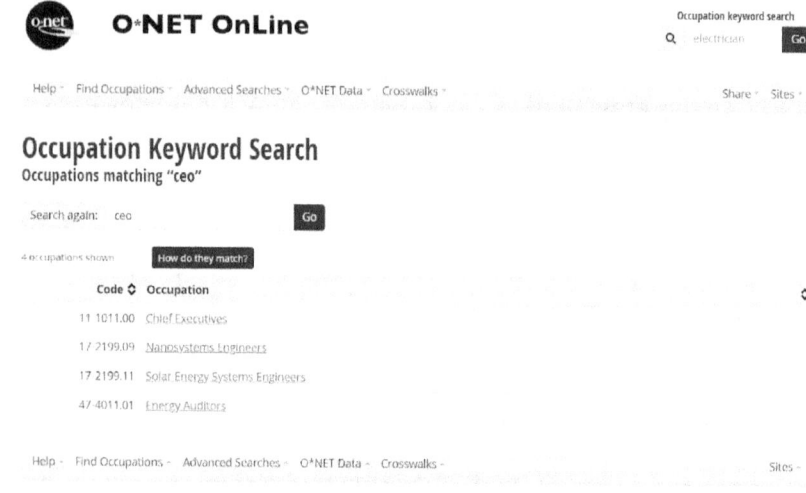

O*NET Online sample search results

After clicking on the Chief Executives link, I was brought to the following page. If you scroll down you will get to this description of skills, knowledge, and desired education for the job. We can use this information to help us develop Skill Based Subheadings for your resume.

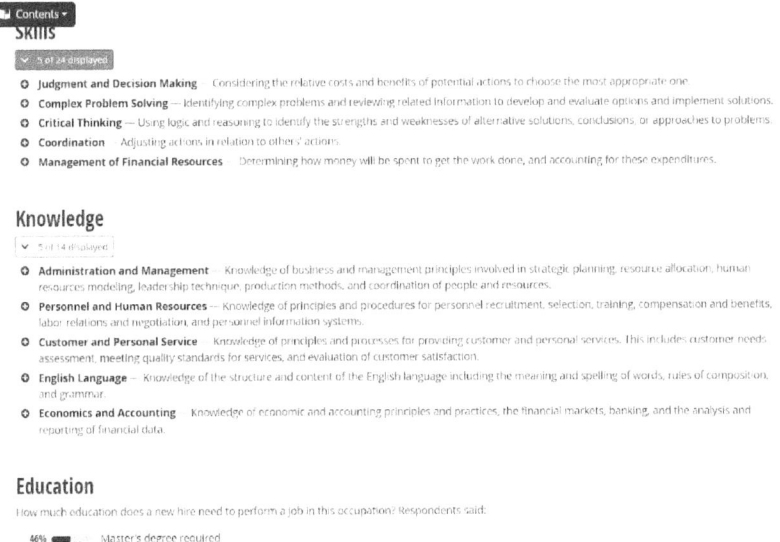

*O*NET Online Position Skill Analysis*

Key Point #9: Use O*NET to better organize your career experiences based on skills, not tasks, and create the motivational push behind your resume.

As you use the O*NET website, you can begin to see what skills and experiences are expected in the type of position you are interested in holding. This is extremely informative for individuals looking to change careers. You may have skills and abilities that are transferable for the current position you hold into the position that you want. As you learn more about your motivation for the next position, you can begin to expose yourself to training and on-the-job experiences that start to give you the skills you need in order to land the type of job you want.

5

Showcasing your Knowledge, Skills, and Abilities

B y now you probably have a number of thoughts swirling in your mind about how you want to attack writing this resume. You probably have ideas about how you want to organize the resume and how you can better organize the experiences under each job listed in your resume when you select the right skill based subheadings.

Now that your outline within an outline is complete, it is time to begin writing the substance of your resume. The chart below is designed to offer some insights on building your resume while also answering some of the frequently asked questions I get as an HR executive.

7 Dos and Don'ts for Resume Writing

DO

1. Research the type of job you want and the skills you need for that job. Include information about those skills in jobs you had through your career.

2. Create additional white space in your resume by creating skill based subheadings
3. Use bullets to further increase white space and describe your work experiences keeping each bullet to no more than 3-6 lines
4. Use action words to lead off each bullet and change the action words you use. You can find a number of action words organized by skill on using the online article for 185+ Best Action Verbs by *The Muse* (see Resources)
5. Include what you achieved by the actions you took on the job
6. Share relevant information about volunteer activities that relate to the job you want
7. Review and edit your work by having someone you trust offer feedback on your resume

DON'T

1. Create a "word wall" full of long paragraphs to describe your job experiences
2. Copy your job description and use it for your resume. Employers are not interested in job tasks. They want to know what your skills and achievements are
3. Lie about your accomplishments or experiences
4. Use statements that contain "we". The resume is about your individual professional accomplishments. Limit the use of "we" in interviews as well.
5. Include periods of unemployment unless specifically asked in the job application
6. Put the year you graduated from high school, college, etc. if it has been more than five years. This helps avoid telling how much your higher education has aged.
7. Overuse Artificial Intelligence to generate too much of your

resume. Writing skill is a sought after ability for employers. Knowing the story you wrote will help you have confidence during the interview.

Key Point #10: A resume is not a position description. A resume is a marketing document highlighting your unique knowledge, skills, and abilities to get the interview for the job you want.

The "So What" Approach

One of the biggest don'ts I listed above is related to key point #11. Too often I see job applicants just dump their position description into the resume, which does not make a compelling case for you to be hired. These types of resumes are lifeless and often fail when put in front of a recruiter or hiring official that needs to determine who to select for an interview.

Position description resumes may be easier for you as the resume writer, but you do not want to show in your resume that you take so little pride in yourself and the work you do. It is okay if you start with your job description, just do not end the resume writing there. You can easily add your spin to your job experience by asking yourself the question "So what?".

- You created reports for the shareholder's meeting. So what?
- You designed floor plans for office configurations. So what?
- You assisted customers at the cash register. So what?

Asking yourself this question is designed to help you uncover why what you do matters. Sharing this information in your resume will also help potential employers to understand why or how it is important as well.

26

Answering this question in the bullets you write also demonstrates creativity, which is a quality that all employers want. The goal with asking "so what" is to help you connect to something larger than just the tasks written down in your position description. The answers to this question help you to see how you made a difference, no matter how big or small that difference was.

Key Point #11: All employers are interested in learning ways you did something faster, better, or cheaper. Showcase your experience using these three perspectives.

Faster, Better, Cheaper

The follow up answers to the "so what" question can be made easier if you think about how you did something faster, better, or cheaper. What employer doesn't want someone who is fast, or finds better ways of doing something, or creates savings in time or money spent? Every bullet in your resume will not always be able to demonstrate a Faster, Better, Cheaper outcome, but you will be surprised how many can include this information.

The easiest of the three to share is usually the "better" component. "Better" is rooted in the concept of continuous improvement as it relates to processes or business practices. The "Better" component also allows you to use data to showcase how you improved your work or your work team's performance overall. The "Better" component can be combined to demonstrate a faster or cheaper outcome. Better can also be about improving the experience of customers.

The one area that I encourage anyone who has had a customer service job to focus on is how you improved customer experience. Most businesses are customer- centric and rely on growing their customer base to become more profitable and create jobs. Showcasing how you understand the concept of customer experience and what drives high satisfaction is a transferable skill to any job you may have whether your customer is the general public or individuals within your own organization (i.e. supervisor, executives, co-workers, etc.).

Key Point #12: Having an understanding of the impact of customer experience concepts can be a game changer for a resume.

Customer experience actually mirrors aspects of the faster, better, cheaper concept in some easy. Customer experience at its core is about three things:

- How easy something is for the customer (faster)
- How efficient (quick or on-time) or effective (accurate) your customer solutions are (faster and better)
- How good the customer feels about the service you delivered

While it is easy to claim that you made things easy or efficient for the customer, it is more important that you include how you achieved those feelings for the customer and/or how you know you achieved those outcomes. You can do this by structuring your bullets using the Task, Action, Outcome (TAO) approach to bullet writing.

Task, Action, Outcome (TAO) Bullet Writing

When structuring your bullets, they too, should be organized and have a beginning, middle, and end. Ensuring you have all three components in as many bullets as you can will set you apart from your competition for the job, especially when you get to the interview.

As we have mentioned before, the resume is about marketing your experiences. Using the TAO process upfront allows you to not only market your experiences, but it starts to let the employer know how you will fit into the culture of the organization.

Job fit is almost as important as what you know. Using the TAO approach can help employers see how what you do can fit into their organization even before the interview is conducted. You can then use the highlights you offered in your resume to tell a fuller story in the job interview.

Earlier in this chapter, I shared the following bullet:

- *Assisted customers at the cash register.*

Using the TAO approach, we can flip this statement to be more complete and show why and how this activity matters. Let's take a look at how to give this bullet more complete structure using the TAO approach coded below:

- Complete point of sale transactions employing courteous customer service techniques for an average of 75 customers per day while handling over $6,000 in sales **to gain repeat customers requesting me by name to complete their future transactions.**

Plain text = Task Underlined text = Action Bold text = Outcome

Maybe you worked in the food service industry and had customers return to get served by you or wanted to know the days you worked so they could interact with you again. Maybe you received consistent "5-star" customer reviews of your work and they wanted to use your service again in the future because of how you treated them or how they felt good after their interaction with you.

While this example above shows the TAO approach in order, so long as you have each component in the bullet, you are effectively using the TAO approach. You could easily flip the order of the bullet to start with the Action or the Outcome instead of the Task as shown below:

- <u>Employ courteous customer service techniques for an average of 75 customers per day while handling over $6,000 in sales</u> when completing point of sale transactions and **gained repeat customers requesting me by name to complete their future transactions.**

Underlined text = Action
Plain text = Task
Bold text = Outcome

Bottom line, no matter what career field you are in you can use the TAO approach to deepen the information you share in the resume to make it more complete. Creating more complete bullets can shorten the resume in some cases as you concentrate your efforts on conveying why and/or how your work experiences are meaningful or made a difference.

More importantly, it will leave reviewers of your resume feeling more "zen" as they can easily find reasons why you deserve to be brought in for an interview. In the interview you can then tell stories about what "courteous customer service" looks like and what it means to you. You could share about how customers have come up to and told you why they keep choosing to come back and interact with you.

Key Point #13: Using the Task, Action, Outcome (TAO) approach helps showcase how to be a strong ambassador for yourself, and foreshadows how you can be a strong ambassador for your potential employer.

6

Resume Layouts and Editing

As an HR executive I have seen a diverse approach to resume writing. I have seen all different kinds of layouts. I have read about the importance of the color and weight of the paper you use. I have seen resumes with photos of the job candidate on the first page that took up more room than their job experience. I have also received resumes with perfume and cologne on them. All these efforts are done with one thing in mind: stand out.

I cannot dispute that a resume on pink paper did make it easier to find. I personally know individuals who received internships based on their looks. The truth of the matter is we are now in the age of artificial intelligence and electronic communication. The importance now is on what you say in your resume, not how it is printed, for the vast majority of resumes.

While it can be important to present a professional looking resume if you are at a job fair, putting so much effort into designing the perfect resume template and what colors you should use is becoming less and less important.

Differences between Industries

Some industries may have a particular format or information that they want to see in the resumes they receive. Some companies may prefer a competency based resume that focuses on skills you bring to the organization not who you worked for. I have also seen companies request an accomplishment resume that focused solely on your accomplishments in your field. These requests, though, are atypical. Most companies will still accept and hire people who submit resumes in a more traditional format.

A traditional resume is essentially 3-5 pages long, uses standard margins of about 1 inch, or 2.5 centimeters, all around, and uses 11-12 point type, when printed. Sticking with a resume in a standard format while utilizing the writing plan you learned in this book will help ensure that you stand out. Using this format makes it easier for the recruiter, or the artificial intelligence robot, to understand how you are qualified for the position you applied for.

One thing you may not know is that depending on the industry, the type and amount of information the employer requests in your resume can be quite different. I can think of no bigger difference in information requests when it comes to the comparison of a resume submitted to a private sector compared to a resume submitted for a Federal Government job.

A Word on Federal Government Resumes and Applications

You may not be accustomed to sharing some of the information as requested in a federal government resume, but it is important that you understand one key difference in customizing your resume for jobs with the Federal Government. The HR office could designate your resume as ineligible, or delay its review, if you do not provide all the information they request as part of the job vacancy posting.

Additionally, Federal government pay is very structured. Offering the salary information and hours worked upfront can help you request and lock in a higher salary if you are selected for the position. Additionally, the Federal government offers some insights to resume writing and how to navigate their job postings so you can include all the information they require.

Specifically, the Federal Government must post all their jobs on the internet by federal law. Their job site is located at www.usajobs.gov. This is the government's job search engine. If you find a job you would like to apply for, make sure you check under the "How to Apply" section of the job announcement so you know if there are any special information requirements that the position is requesting.

In Figure 1 and Figure 2 below, you can see a couple of photos of the Federal government's optional resume form called the Optional Form (OF) 612. This form is now obsolete, because the government has a self guided resume builder. You can also use your own resume to apply, but, it is possible you could leave out key information from your resume and delay your application for the position you want to interview for (see Figure 2)

OPTIONAL APPLICATION FOR FEDERAL EMPLOYMENT - OF 612

OMB No. 3206-0219

You may apply for most jobs with a resume, this form, or other written format. If your resume or application does not provide all the information requested on this form and in the job vacancy announcement, you may lose consideration for a job.

Figure 1 showing information often requested for federal government resumes that are usually not part of a private sector resume. Also important to note that nearly all jobs for the U.S. Federal Government require you to be a U.S. citizen.

PRIVACY ACT AND PUBLIC BURDEN STATEMENTS

35

Figure 2 showing page 2 of the OF-612 form indicating the laws in place that require federal government agencies to request this information. Pay special attention to the circled area, as an example.

I strongly recommend creating a Federal Government style resume if you are interested in working in the government sector so you can have various options for potential job opportunities to choose from. The Government's regimented approach to hiring can cause delays in response time, so don't consider that delay to be a reflection on your resume or skills, especially if you provided all the information they requested.

Federal agencies hire over 250,000 people each year and can receive thousands of resumes for a single position. A real person is required to check the work of their automated tools before referring candidates to the hiring official. This increases the chance of your resume being viewed by a real person and recognizing the organization and detail you included, which will set you apart from most other job applicants.

Editing and Finalizing

Once you have written your resume draft, I encourage you to give it to someone else to review. Their fresh eyes will help find grammatical errors you may have missed. Sharing your resume will also allow you to ask how the person felt when reading through your resume.

- Were they impressed?
- Were they confused?
- Were there areas where they wanted to know more about your job experience?
- Were there areas where they thought you could streamline your

resume?

If you ask these questions when requesting their honest feedback, it can help you hone your resume further before sending it off to your dream job.

7

Conclusion

G reat resumes are usually the result of great organization. I can think of no better time investment than ensuring that you position yourself for the best possible outcome when applying for that new job. Having a great resume also sets you up for success in the job interview that is sure to follow.

First, if you found the information in this book helpful, please take some time to offer your feedback by offering your review on Amazon, Audible, or whatever book reading interface you chose to use. I would greatly appreciate it and thank you in advance for sharing.

Second, keep in mind my 7 Dos and Don'ts for writing your resume.

Finally, lean on the baker's dozen of key points below to share clarity about your professional motivation and purpose as you create your winning resume.

Key Point #1: The true purpose of resume writing is to focus your efforts on ways you can unlock, uncover, and unleash your unique story.

Key Point #2: Everyone has a story to tell, and the resume is your tool to create that story and inspire others with your unique professional story.

Key Point #3: Your main role as the author of your resume is to provide the resume reader a map of your expertise and experiences by making it easy to understand your expertise and achievements.

Key Point #4: Having a Relevant Volunteer Work Experience section in your resume is also a great way to showcase another dimension of your personality.

Key Point #5: It is a rare circumstance that your level of education will be the sole determining factor as to why you get hired.

Key Point #6: If you can speak another language and could pass an assessment that tests your fluency, you need to put that on your resume.

Key Point #7: Showcasing awards demonstrates that your expertise is valued and recognized by entities outside of your current office while showing a connection with a broader community of interest to your prospective employer.

Key point #8: Your resume is actually the script for your job interview.

Key Point #9: Use O*NET to better organize your career experiences based on skills, not tasks, and create the motivational push behind your resume.

Key Point #10: A resume is not a position description. A resume is a marketing document highlighting your unique knowledge, skills, and abilities to get the interview for the job you want.

Key Point #11: All employers are interested in learning ways you did *something faster, better, or cheaper. Showcase your experience using these three perspectives.*

Key Point #12: Having an understanding of the impact of customer experience concepts can be a game changer for a resume.

Key Point #13: Using the Task, Action, Outcome (TAO) approach helps showcase how to be a strong ambassador for yourself, and foreshadows how you can be a strong ambassador for your potential employer in the future.

I really enjoyed sharing my insight with you, which I have used to reach to the highest levels of my own profession. Thank you for choosing to use this book as a tool to further your own career aspirations.

8

Resources

The *World's First Resume is 500-years Old and Still Can Teach You a Lesson or Two*. (n.d.). https://www.linkedin.com/business/talent/blog/talent-acquisition/worlds-first-resume-is-500-years-old#Would%20Da%20Vinci%E2%80%99s%20Resume%20Work%20Today?

Accessions Trend (FY 2020 - FY 2024) - IBM Cognos PowerPlay Studio. (n.d.). https://www.fedscope.opm.gov/ibmcognos/bi/v1/disp?b_action=powerPlayService&m_encoding=UTF-8&BZ=1AAABuwvODpp42pVOwW6DMAz9mZi2h1WOEyY4cEgIqBwGXeGy08RoOlVjMBH_X1NAW7fd9p4s2c%7EPTw7qal831SkrTOLmcbKF2QLRVcsoirlOBXKUEQpleIYm5CKWRut7CUS7wN9m6pQejqo5JEB5Nw6zHWag%7EDL2ZztBqEHi0L5bEGZzbLu39tW6Z9V11rnrOLgNhAYo%7E1g3v_03FxA2kx3OQLjNn4DQEwjvgPBrljufFZg63adVWWZpU1RlqR6y5L85gX5MLoiMIyLnyBhDFiIjZJ6MfeeBP%7EZhqu8BY9PO9o%7EEEgCIggUCWA70AxavAbwJbACS8%7EQf4wqVbf1lq%7EEWDFJ1yrbck%3D

Optional forms. (n.d.). U.S. Office of Personnel Management. https://www.opm.gov/forms/Optional-forms/

The Muse. (2023, December 14). *185+ Best Action Verbs to Impress Hiring Managers in 2024.* https://www.themuse.com/advice/185-powerful-verbs-that-will-make-your-resume-awesome